DNA

Alvin Silverstein, Virginia Silverstein, and Laura Silverstein Nunn

TFCB Twenty-First Century Books
Minneapolis

Twenty-First Century Books
A division of Lerner Publishing Group, Inc.
241 First Avenue North
Minneapolis, MN 55401 U.S.A.

Website address: www.lernerbooks.com

Library of Congress Cataloging-in-Publication Data

Silverstein, Alvin.
    DNA / by Alvin Silverstein, Virginia Silverstein, Laura Silverstein Nunn. —
Rev. ed.
        p.   cm. — (Science concepts, second series)
    Includes bibliographical references and index.
    ISBN 978–0–8225–8654–8 (lib. bdg. : alk. paper)
    1. DNA—Juvenile literature. I. Silverstein, Virginia B. II. Nunn, Laura
Silverstein. III. Title.
    QP624.S55 2009
    572.8'6—dc22   2007048819

Manufactured in the United States of America
1 2 3 4 5 6 – DP – 14 13 12 11 10 09

Contents

chapter one

The Code of Life

Why does a dog have puppies and not kittens? Why do a hen's eggs hatch into chicks instead of ducklings? Why does an acorn grow into an oak tree instead of a sunflower? And why does a human give birth to a human baby rather than to a baby horse? All these living things follow the laws of nature.

While the various creatures on Earth may seem different, they all have something in common: each living thing is made up of tiny units, called cells. Cells are the building blocks of life. Just as bricks are stacked to build a wall, cells are the bricks that build a living creature. The larger the organism, the more cells it contains.

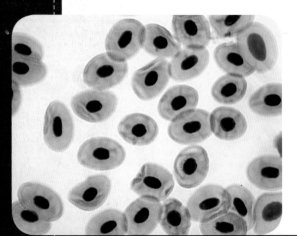

These cells make up the blood of a frog.

Like all animals, these elephants are made up of cells. As the baby elephant gets older, its body produces more cells and grows larger.

So in a sense, all living things—from a tiny ant to a flowering dogwood tree to an enormous whale—share a common thread: the cells that compose them. And yet, there are distinct differences. A mouse looks very different from an elephant, and a spider in no way, shape, or form resembles a giraffe. Even creatures within the same species look different from one another. You would not confuse a Great Dane with a Chihuahua or a dachshund. And you most likely do not look like any of your friends.

Did You Know?

Your body is made up of trillions of cells. Can you imagine how many cells there are in the largest creature on Earth, the blue whale? It can grow to more than 100 feet (30 meters) long!

Your Instruction Manual

If all living things have cells in common, then what makes organisms so different? The key is what's inside the cells: genetic material, called DNA (deoxyribonucleic acid). DNA is the working part of the chromosomes, small rodlike structures in cells that contain genes, the units of heredity. Genes carry the information that determines the characteristics of a cell and the instructions for making new cells. Many new cells are formed as a baby grows into an adult. New cells are also formed when different parts of the body are damaged and need repair.

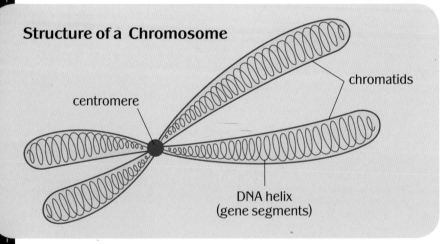

Structure of a Chromosome

chromatids

centromere

DNA helix
(gene segments)

This is the structure of a chromosome in a cell preparing to divide. The cell has copied all of its DNA, and each chromosome exists in the form of two rod-shaped parts, called chromatids. The two identical chromatids contain DNA—genetic material—coiled into a spiral, or helix. The centromere holds the two chromatids together.

The information in DNA is "written" in a special chemical code. Each living thing has a unique code. Scientists have been learning to read the DNA code. They are using this knowledge to help treat diseases that are caused by genetic errors. Uncovering the mysteries of DNA has also helped scientists trace our ancestry. DNA has even become a useful tool in solving crimes.

Although the differences in genetic code make us quite diverse, most of the code is almost exactly the same in all living things—viruses, bacteria, plants, animals, and humans. In fact, the code of life, which holds the secrets to all our differences, also holds the answer to the many ways in which all forms of life are so much alike.

Back in the 1800s, before telephones, radios,

satellites, or the Internet existed, people could

communicate across great distances by telegraph.

Telegraph messages were sent by tapping out a code

that involved only two symbols, dot (·) and dash (−). In

Morse code (named after Samuel Morse, the inventor

of the telegraph), these two signs can spell out any

word or sentence in the English language.

The language of DNA is spelled out in a code that is a bit more complicated than Morse code. It uses a four-letter chemical alphabet. These chemical letters are combined in a special order to form "words," "sentences," and "paragraphs," all linked together in long DNA chains. The DNA in each cell is like a recipe book, divided into a number of "chapters" (the chromosomes). Within each chapter are a number of individual recipes—the genes. Each gene holds the instructions for making a specific product. The same four letters can combine in many different ways to spell out many different traits in an organism.

The DNA Model

The nucleic part of deoxyribonucleic acid means that DNA is found mainly in the nucleus of a cell. The nucleus is the cell's control center. It contains the genetically coded instructions for the cell's activities, including growth and reproduction. All these instructions are spelled out in the chromosomes, in the chemical units that make up DNA.

DNA is a long, threadlike chain of chemical units called nucleotides, each consisting of three parts: a phosphate, a sugar (deoxyribose), and a substance called a nitrogen base. The sugar phosphates link together to form a chain. (They are the backbone of the chain.) The nitrogen bases stick out and can react with other bases on a different chain. So DNA is actually a double chain, consisting of two long strings (strands) of nucleotides linked together by chemical bonds between nitrogen bases.

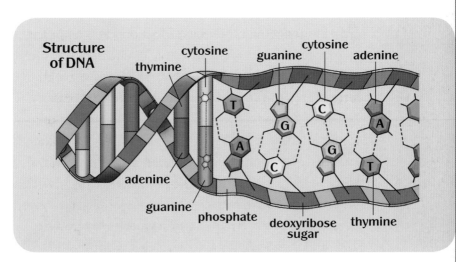

This is the structure of DNA. Adenine, thymine, guanine, and cytosine are the four kinds of nitrogen bases found in DNA.

James Watson (left) *and Francis Crick* (right) *display their model of a DNA molecule.*

The DNA molecule is curled in a spiral, or helix. It looks like a spiral staircase, with the nitrogen bases forming the steps and the sugar phosphates forming the sides. This double helix model of the DNA molecule was first worked out in 1953 by a British biochemist, Francis Crick, and his American colleague, James Watson.

Four kinds of nitrogen bases are found in DNA: adenine, thymine, guanine, and cytosine. (Usually abbreviated as A, T, G, and C, they are the four letters of the DNA alphabet.) They bond with one another according to very specific rules: A always pairs with T, and C pairs with G. So if you have a sequence on one strand such as ATCGTTA, then the corresponding part of the other strand will be TAGCAAT. Normally, when scientists talk about a base sequence of DNA, they are referring to one strand. Once you know the order of the bases in one strand, the pairing rules automatically tell you the sequence in the other.

Generally, each gene directs the production of a protein. The proteins direct chemical reactions inside the cell or form body structures. DNA's instructions, expressed in the form of proteins, determine the traits of each organism. These instructions are spelled out in the four-letter alphabet of DNA's nitrogen bases, which is translated into amino acids, the building blocks of proteins.

Twenty different kinds of amino acids exist. When the right kinds of amino acids are put together in the right amounts, they make a protein. Like Morse code and the English alphabet, the four DNA bases and the twenty different amino acids can be used in many combinations to spell out a huge number of words. For example, one combination of

This computer model shows chains of amino acids forming the spiral protein threads in a molecule from a red blood cell.

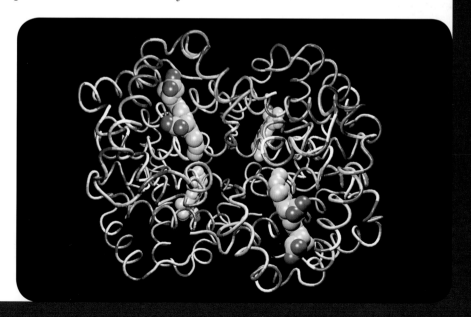

amino acids might spell out a protein called keratin, which forms your hair and fingernails.

How is the four-letter alphabet of DNA turned into the twenty-letter alphabet of the amino acids? A single gene is spelled out in mixtures of three letters. Each corresponds to one amino acid in a protein. The three-letter sequences are called codons. To translate DNA's message into proteins, the codons are first copied into another kind of nucleic acid, RNA (ribonucleic acid).

Just Junk?

Genes are not lined up along the DNA chain like the beads of a necklace. Actually, chromosomes are a lot more complex than that. Only a small portion of each DNA molecule—as little as 1.2 percent—consists of genes. There are long stretches of base pairs that are not translated into proteins. For a long time, scientists thought these parts of DNA were just taking up space. They labeled them junk DNA. Some of these seemingly useless strings of base pairs are found between genes, like the spacers between beads on a necklace. Other bits of "junk" are actually inserted into the genes themselves. These inserted pieces, called introns, are like the commercial breaks in a TV show. They interrupt the story, which is

RNA's Role

As you know, the DNA's job is to store the master plans for everything that goes on in a living organism. But without RNA, these plans could never be carried out.

Like DNA, RNA is a long spiral chain made up of links containing a sugar, a phosphate, and a nitrogen base. The sugar is ribose, which is very similar to the deoxyribose in DNA. Three of the four bases (A, C, and G) are the same as those found in DNA. The fourth base is U (uracil), which is similar to but not exactly the same as the T (thymine) in DNA.

---

told by exons—the parts of the gene attached to the introns. When a cell makes working copies of a gene, the introns are snipped out so that only the chain of exons remains. This is like editing out the commercials when watching a TV show.

What is all that junk DNA doing there? Scientists are finding that not all of it is as useless as it seems. Some of it spells out controls and switches that influence how the nearby genes work. Some parts seem to be leftovers from long-ago ancestors. They are like "ghost genes" that got changed during evolution (the gradual change of living things over thousands of years). They no longer contain instructions the cell can read. And some of the junk DNA may serve as raw material for new genes that may be useful in the future.

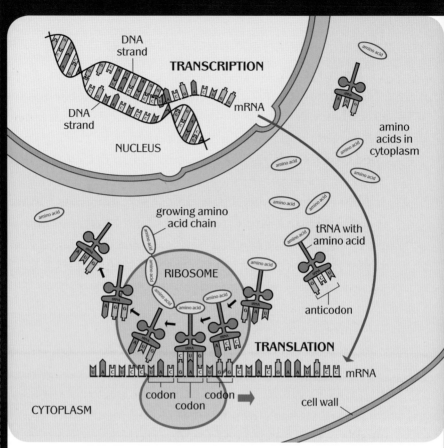

This diagram shows how RNA uses the information encoded in DNA to create proteins in ribosomes. First, part of the DNA in the nucleus is copied into messenger RNA, which moves out into the cytoplasm. This is the pattern that will determine what protein will be made. Messenger RNA pairs up with ribosomal RNA at a ribosome. Small, clover-shaped transfer RNA molecules pick up amino acids from the cytoplasm and carry them to the ribosome. As messenger RNA moves along the ribosome, transfer RNA molecules match up to its three-letter codons, and the amino acids they carry are joined into a growing protein chain. When a "stop signal" codon is reached, the process stops, and the protein drops off.

Unlike DNA, RNA has only a single strand of nucleotides. Its nitrogen bases can form chemical bonds, just like the DNA bases, but they normally do not link two RNA strands together. Instead, working RNA molecules form temporary bonds, either with parts of other RNA molecules or with parts of the DNA sequence.

The bases in RNA follow the same pairing rules as those in DNA: A pairs with U (or with a T in DNA), and G pairs with C. When part of a DNA molecule is copied into RNA, the corresponding RNA bases are linked together. For example, if a portion of the base sequence on DNA is ACTTGA, the RNA copy will have UGAACU.

Three kinds of RNA help DNA translate its message into proteins: messenger RNA, ribosomal RNA, and transfer RNA. Here's how they work. Parts of the DNA—genes— are continually turned on and off as the nucleus receives chemical messages from the rest of the cell and the world outside. The turned-on parts are copied into pieces of RNA that move out into the cytoplasm, the jellylike fluid outside the nucleus. This kind of RNA is called messenger RNA. The DNA message it carries is a set of instructions for making a protein. Messenger RNA waits at tiny ball-like structures called ribosomes, the centers for making proteins, while amino acids are brought to it.

How do all the right amino acids get to the ribosomes and line up on the messenger RNA to put them together? The cell has a special taxicab service to carry them there. The taxicabs are molecules of a different kind of RNA— transfer RNA.

Transfer RNA molecules are much smaller than the

messenger RNAs, and their job is much simpler. Messenger RNA carries the plans for a whole long protein molecule. But transfer RNA just has to pick up its own special amino acid and find its place on the messenger RNA molecule. It does this by matching up parts of the base sequence.

The ribosomes have their own RNA—ribosomal RNA. This third type of RNA lines up the long messenger RNA molecules and helps match them

Cracking the Code

By the beginning of the 1960s, scientists had figured out that three-letter codons in DNA and RNA determine which amino acids will be built into proteins, but nobody knew exactly how the code worked. If you write down all the possible three-letter combinations in an alphabet of four letters (such as the A, U, C, and G in RNA), you will find that there are sixty-four of them. But there are only twenty different amino acids in most proteins. Are all the possible codons used? That would mean that more than one codon can correspond to the same amino acid.

In 1961 Marshall Nirenberg and J. Heinrich Matthaei made an artificial strand of RNA out of pure uracil up with the right transfer RNA taxicabs carrying their amino acid passengers.

This is where those three-letter codons come in. As a protein starts to form, the end of a messenger RNA becomes attached to a ribosome. A transfer RNA molecule with a three-letter base sequence matching the first codon of the "message" lines up next to it, bringing its amino acid. Then the ribosome begins to move down the messenger RNA chain.

and placed it in a solution of amino acids. The artificial RNA (poly-U) quickly made a protein by stringing together molecules of just one amino acid, phenylalanine. So the codon UUU corresponds to phenylalanine. Other scientists quickly began making artificial RNA molecules and checking what amino acids each possible codon specified. By 1965 the entire genetic code had been worked out. Sixty-one of the sixty-four possible codons correspond to specific amino acids. The other three are "stop" signals that tell the ribosome to stop adding amino acids to the protein.

The genetic code allows for small errors in copying without any great harm to the protein. For example, if the codon GGU is miscopied, substituting an A for the U, it won't matter—the codon will still specify the same amino acid, glycine.

> ### Did You Know?
> Human cells can make more than one hundred thousand different kinds of proteins designed to do many jobs all over the body.

Each time a space opens up, a transfer RNA with three nucleotides matching the next codon of the message moves in to fill it. Soon a whole row of transfer RNA molecules is lined up next to messenger RNA. Each one is holding an amino acid. The amino acids link together to form a chain of their own—a protein molecule. The sequence of amino acids in the new protein is determined by the sequence of bases in the messenger RNA. And it is the sequence of amino acids in the protein that decides what kind of protein it will be.

The growing protein molecule looks like a dangling tail as the ribosome moves on. Finally, the ribosome gets to the end of the messenger RNA molecule and drops off. The new protein molecule breaks away and goes off to do its job in the cell.

When Cells Divide

You started your life as a single cell. That cell divided and divided again and then became a ball of cells. As it got bigger, parts of it started to change. Soon a distinct head, body, and little tail grew. Eventually, buds on the sides grew into arms and legs. Meanwhile, the body grew and the tail disappeared.

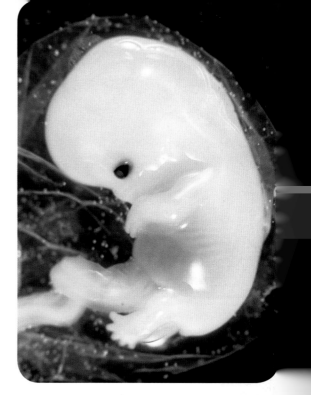

The cells of the human embryo above have divided only a few times. All the cells look the same. But at four weeks old, the embryo (right) has distinct cells in its eyes, skin, and internal organs.

Eyes, ears, nose, and mouth formed on the head. Inside the body, internal organs developed: a beating heart, lungs that weren't working yet, stomach, and all the other structures that make up a human being.

For nine months, you grew and developed inside your mother's body. Even after you were born, you continued to get bigger, and you will continue to grow and develop through your teen years. Through all this growth, from the first cell to a baby, a child, and finally an adult, the number of cells in the body increases. This happens by cell division. In this process, a single cell grows and splits into two cells.

Even after growth has stopped, cell division is still important. When cells get injured or wear out, they need to be replaced. That's how you can heal when you cut your finger or break a bone. Also certain cells are constantly being produced. For instance, every time you touch something, you shed dead skin cells. Skin cells live for only about twenty-eight days. When they die, they have to be replaced by new skin cells. Red blood cells also have a short life span. They live for only a few months and need to be replaced regularly.

Each new cell must have its own complete copy of DNA instructions. That means that all the DNA must be copied before cell division takes place. First, the coiled ladder of the DNA molecule starts to uncoil. The two sides then split down the middle at one end, like unzipping a zipper. The steps of the ladder, with their pairings of A with T and C with G are broken apart, leaving them without their partners. They are not alone for long. Floating freely around in the nucleus of the cell are As, Cs, Ts, and Gs. These bases are chemically drawn to their partners on the DNA strand. An enzyme, a special protein that helps start chemical reactions, acts as a matchmaker, bringing the right bases together.

As each base finds its partner—A with T and C with G—they hook up, forming the steps on the DNA ladder. Then two identical DNA molecules exist where once one existed. Each new DNA molecule has one old strand and one newly built one. Each molecule can then twist itself back into a tightly coiled structure. The DNA reproduction process is called replication.

DNA Replication

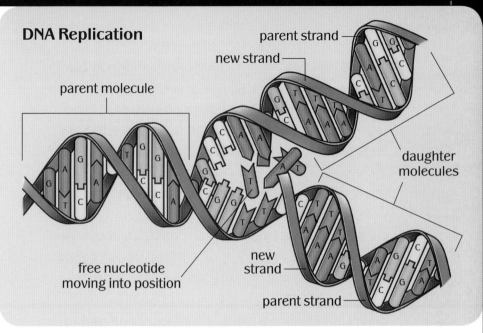

parent strand

new strand

parent molecule

daughter molecules

free nucleotide moving into position

new strand

parent strand

When DNA copies itself, the original strands of DNA split apart to generate new complementary strands. The original DNA is called the parent molecule. The two new DNA chains, each containing one old strand and one new strand, are called daughter molecules.

Basically the same processes are used in making RNA copies of portions of DNA, but only part of the DNA is unzipped and only one strand is copied. When a portion of the DNA molecule is unzipped, RNA nucleotides pair up with the DNA bases and are assembled into a chain. Again, C pairs with G, but A pairs with U when RNA is being formed.

chapter three

How Heredity Works

Has anyone ever told you, "You look just like your father" or "You have your mother's blue eyes"? If you look through your family album, you may notice that you also have your grandmother's curly hair or your uncle's nose. It is true that we are all different—we look different, we sound different, and we act differently. But all members in a family, from the ancient past to the present, may share some similarities.

Whether it's the shape of your nose or your bone structure, parts of you could date back for generations. That's because all living things pass on their code of life—DNA—from generation to generation. You inherited DNA information from both your mother and your father. The DNA you received from your mother and father, in turn, contained information from their parents and so on.

Creating a New Life

Not all living things have a mother and a father. Take single-celled organisms, such as bacteria.

DNA carries the information that determines how a person looks. Some children look a lot like one parent, while others look like a combination of both parents. Some children may even resemble a grandparent.

When it comes to reproduction, a bacterium is more like a copy machine. First, the bacterium copies all of its DNA. Then it splits in half, forming two daughter cells. Usually the two daughter cells are identical twins—two cells that are exact copies of their parent, only smaller. With a complete set of genes and just the right building blocks, the two daughter cells can grow, and the cycle starts all over again.

This E. coli *bacterium has divided into two identical daughter cells.*

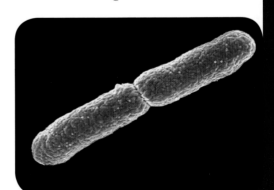

More complex organisms, including humans, go from one generation to the next by sexual reproduction. In this process, a male and a female from the same species combine some of their genetic material. Each of them produces special sex cells used only for reproduction. The sex cells of a female are called eggs, or ova. Those of the male are called sperm.

In humans, all body cells (except the egg and sperm cells) have two sets of twenty-three chromosomes, making a total of forty-six. These chromosomes come in pairs—each chromosome in one set has a matching chromosome in the other set. The two chromosomes in a pair carry genes for the same traits. These genes are arranged in the same order along the two DNA molecules.

Unlike normal body cells, egg cells and sperm cells have only one set of twenty-three chromosomes. So they have only one copy of each gene. When an egg and a sperm join to form the first cell of a new human being, the two sets of chromosomes (twenty-three from each parent) are combined. This joining of two sex cells is called fertilization. The new cell (a fertilized egg) has forty-six chromosomes, a full set of DNA. One set of genes is from the mother, and one set is from the father. So the new organism is not exactly like its mother or just like its father. Instead, it has a mixture of both of its parents' genes. As a result, a new, unique person is born.

When the chromosome sets are divided during the formation of sex cells, it is pure luck which one of each chromosome pair will go to a particular egg or sperm. The result is that each sex cell winds up with a mixed half set of chromosomes—some that came from the father (the grandfather of the new offspring) and some from the mother (the new offspring's grandmother). When an egg and sperm combine, they bring together a mixture of traits from all four

A sperm cell fertilizes an egg cell, combining sets of genes from the mother and the father.

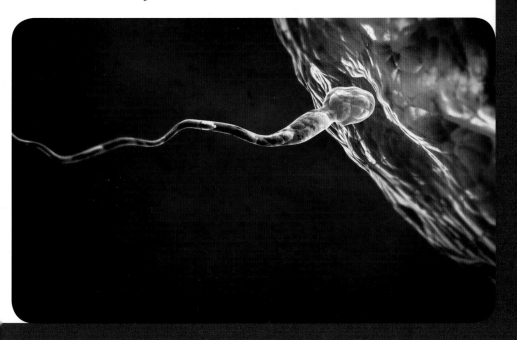

grandparents. That is why children in the same family usually look rather similar but not exactly alike (unless they are identical twins, formed from the same fertilized egg).

Boy or Girl?

When people are expecting a baby, the big question is, "Will it be a boy or a girl?" Actually, that's up to the father. The half set of chromosomes that he provides determines the sex of the baby. In fact, just one of his chromosomes makes the difference.

Most of the chromosomes are the same in both males and females. The difference lies in one special pair of chromosomes, called sex chromosomes. There are two sex chromosomes: the X chromosome and the Y chromosome.

In females, body cells contain two X chromosomes, which look exactly the same in size and shape. Males' sex chromosomes are not a matching pair. Their body cells have one X chromosome and a smaller Y chromosome. When the sex cells form, half of the sperm cells have an X chromosome and the other half have a Y chromosome. If a sperm carrying an X chromosome joins with an egg cell (which has its own X chromosome), then the offspring will be female (XX). But if a sperm carrying a Y chromosome joins with an egg cell, then the offspring will be male (XY).

A Look at Cloning

What if people could reproduce the way bacteria do, making exact copies of themselves? Many science-fiction writers have used this idea since the 1930s. But in 1996, science fiction became fact. Scottish researchers produced a lamb using the DNA from a body cell of an adult sheep. Dolly, the lamb, was a clone, basically an identical twin of her "mother," the DNA donor.

The researchers had inserted the nucleus from her mother's cell into an egg cell from another sheep, after destroying the egg cell's own nucleus. Then they transplanted the egg cell into the uterus of an unrelated surrogate mother sheep. Inside the egg, genes in the nucleus that had been turned off for years were switched on. The egg cell began to grow into an embryo, just as though it were a fertilized egg. Dolly, the clone, developed inside her foster mother's body. But she didn't look at all like her foster mother. Dolly's hereditary instructions came from her genetic mother, the sheep who provided the body-cell nucleus.

Researchers all over the world began to use the new cloning methods. They made clones of a number of other animals,

In 1996, Dolly the lamb became the world's first cloned mammal.

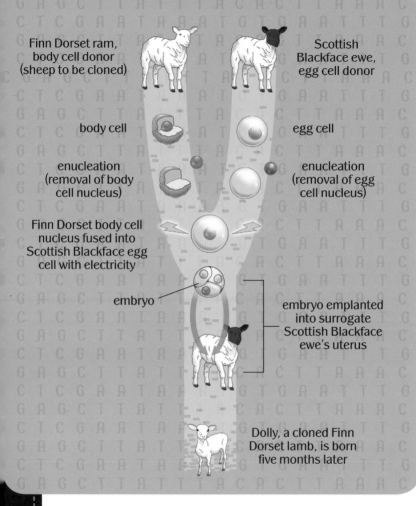

The Cloning of Dolly

Finn Dorset ram, body cell donor (sheep to be cloned)

Scottish Blackface ewe, egg cell donor

body cell

egg cell

enucleation (removal of body cell nucleus)

enucleation (removal of egg cell nucleus)

Finn Dorset body cell nucleus fused into Scottish Blackface egg cell with electricity

embryo

embryo emplanted into surrogate Scottish Blackface ewe's uterus

Dolly, a cloned Finn Dorset lamb, is born five months later

including cows, pigs, horses, cats, dogs, rabbits, and mice. Why would anyone want to clone an animal? It is easy enough to get more cows, pigs, or dogs just by breeding them. But in normal reproduction, you are never sure exactly what you'll get. Each offspring will have a mixture of its mother's and father's traits. A clone, on the other hand, will have exactly the same set of genes as its parent. So breeders could use cloning to make copies of a champion milk-producing cow, for example, or of a sheep with especially soft, thick wool.

Cloning is also a way to make animals that produce large amounts of valuable chemicals for treating diseases. Genes—even human genes—can be added to the embryo before it is transferred to the surrogate mother. The researchers who created Dolly, for example, next made a clone called Polly. Polly produced a human blood-clotting protein in her milk. Other cloned animals make antibodies for treating human diseases.

Cloning may also help save some endangered species. Breeders can grow a cloned embryo in a surrogate mother of a different species. A cloned gaur (an endangered cattle species), for example, grew inside the body of an ordinary cow.

Since the first successful clonings of animals, people have been arguing about whether humans could, would, and should be cloned too. Some people think this would be morally wrong. Others have no problem with the idea. The researchers who produced Dolly say there are some practical reasons why we should not try to clone people. The cloning of mammals is very difficult. Usually it takes hundreds of tries to get a successful clone. Sometimes the clones have birth defects or may have a shortened life span.

Most people believe that we should not clone complete humans. But cloning techniques may be useful in treating illnesses and other medical conditions. For example, organs and tissues could be cloned for transplants. A patient's body would not reject a cloned heart, kidneys, or lungs transplanted to replace original organs that are failing.

Unequal Partners

An Austrian monk named Gregor Mendel discovered the laws of heredity. He studied thousands of pea plants, which he grew in his monastery garden for over ten years starting in 1856. After crossing (mating) plants with different

CopyCat

Many people feel as though their pets are part of the family. But most pets have much shorter life spans than humans. If a pet dies, some people may wish they could have a replacement exactly like the one they loved. In 2002 Texas researchers announced that they had cloned a cat. They named her CC, short for CopyCat.

CC was a healthy kitten who grew into a lively, affectionate house cat. She is not an *exact* copy of her clone-mother, Rainbow. The color and markings of their fur are not quite the same, and Rainbow has a chunkier build. Their personalities are different too—CC is more playful. These differences are the result of their different life histories. Although they share the same genes, they grew up in different surroundings, both before and after birth.

traits, such as green pods and yellow pods, Mendel found that traits are passed along from one generation to the next in tiny little packages, which we call genes. Mendel found that two genes are responsible for each trait. The two genes in a pair may be different. Scientists call different forms of the same gene alleles.

Cloning is a lot more difficult and expensive than normal reproduction. (It took 188 tries to produce CC.) But some pet owners are still tempted. In 2004 a woman in Texas paid fifty thousand dollars for a clone of her cat Nicky, who had died at the age of seventeen the year before. Little Nicky's owner was delighted. Not only did the kitten look just like his genetic parent, but he also acted like him. For example, Little Nicky loves to jump into a bathtub full of water for a swim. The first Nicky also had an unusual liking for water.

Cloning dogs is even harder than cloning cats. But in 2005, South Korean scientists succeeded in cloning an Afghan hound. They named the puppy Snuppy (pronounced Snoopy, for Seoul National University puppy). The researchers weren't trying to replace a family pet. They were more interested in finding ways to cure diseases. Some of the diseases that dogs get are very similar to human diseases.

The alleles that Mendel studied do not act like equal partners. Crossing tall pea plants with short ones, for example, produced only tall offspring. A cross of green and yellow pod plants gave only green pods in the next generation. In each case, one allele seemed to have a stronger influence in determining the traits of the offspring. Mendel called the stronger form dominant. The dominant trait is the one that appeared in the hybrid (mixed) offspring. Mendel used the term *recessive* for the trait that did not show up in the hybrid offspring. The recessive trait reappeared in the next generation when the hybrid plants were crossed.

Later scientists coined the term *phenotype* for the appearance of a trait and *genotype* for the combination of alleles that is responsible for the trait. A dominant trait will show up in the phenotype whether the genotype has one or two of those alleles. A recessive

Gregor Mendel was born in 1822. He is known as the father of modern genetics.

Quirks of Fate

Gregor Mendel is known as the father of modern genetics, but during his lifetime, very few people knew about him and his work. He published his results in the journal of the local natural history society, but they were ignored for over thirty years. Then, in 1900, an amazing coincidence occurred. Three scientists (Hugo de Vries in the Netherlands, Karl Correns in Germany, and Erich von Tschermak-Setsebegg in Austria), each working on their own, came up with a theory of heredity that was very similar to Mendel's. While researching the subject, each scientist read Mendel's publications. All three published their own results as supporting evidence and gave Gregor Mendel full credit for the theory of genetics.

trait will appear, however, only if the recessive allele is inherited from both parents.

The laws that Mendel discovered in experiments on peas hold true for other plants and animals, as well—including humans. For example, if a woman with black hair (who comes from an all-black-haired family) marries a man with blond hair, all their children are likely to have black hair. The phenotype of black hair color is produced by a dark-colored pigment, melanin, and the production of this pigment is a dominant trait. But two black-haired people can have a blond child if they both have a mixed genotype.

Punnett Squares

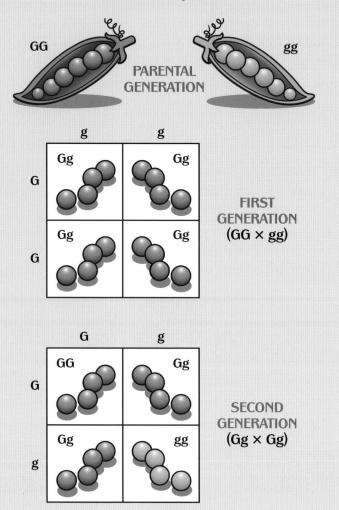

GG

gg

PARENTAL GENERATION

g   g

G | Gg | Gg

G | Gg | Gg

FIRST GENERATION (GG × gg)

G   g

G | GG | Gg

g | Gg | gg

SECOND GENERATION (Gg × Gg)

The expected results of a cross of two different genotypes can be determined by using a simple diagram called a Punnett square. The mother's genotype is at the left, and the father's genotype at the top. The possible combinations in the first and second generations are shown in the four boxes of the squares.

For many traits, the patterns of inheritance are not quite so simple. In some plant species, unlike Mendel's peas, the color of the flowers in hybrid offspring is not like that of the dominant parent. Instead, it is a blending of the colors of the two parents. Purebred plants with red flowers, for example, when crossed with purebred plants with white flowers, give hybrid offspring with pink flowers. In such cases, the dominance of one allele over the other is not complete.

Heredity is also complicated when more than one pair of alleles are involved in determining a trait. A brown-eyed mother and a blue-eyed father, for example, are likely to have children with brown eyes. (Like hair color, dark eye color is produced by melanin.) But the children may have blue eyes (if the mother has a hybrid genotype) or gray, green, or hazel eyes, because the other genes also are involved. At least ten different genes determine human skin color, so children in the same family can have skin of quite different shades. There is even another set of alleles that

In this family, each of the three children has a slightly different combination of their parents' hair, skin, and eye colors.

can influence hair color. A gene for an orange pigment can produce various shades of red hair, depending on how much melanin the hair also contains.

The seven traits that Mendel studied in pea plants are all inherited independently. A tall plant, for example, can have either green or yellow pods and either smooth or wrinkled seeds. So can a short plant. Scientists later discovered that each of the seven traits is on a different one of the pea plant's seven pairs of chromosomes. But what happens if the genes for two traits are on the same chromosome? In the early 1900s, researchers discovered that certain traits always seemed to be inherited together. For example, fruit flies with the usual red eyes have normal-size wings, but fruit flies with white eyes have wings that are much smaller than normal. Soon scientists realized that the genes for these linked traits are found on the same chromosome.

Studies on large numbers of animals and plants show that linked traits are not quite *always* inherited together. In any large number of fruit fly crosses, for example, there will be a few offspring that have white eyes and normal-size wings and a few with red eyes and tiny wings. The reason is that when the chromosomes pair up while a cell is dividing, they temporarily join at the middle. Their dangling ends may cross over each other. Sometimes the chromosomes break at the crossover point. The cell's repair enzymes quickly put them back together, but sometimes they mistakenly attach the broken pieces to the wrong chromosomes. Each chromosome in the pair then has some genes from the mother and some from the father.

Crossing over is thus another way of adding genetic variety to the new offspring. It also gives scientists a tool for determining the relative positions of genes on a chromosome.

A Matter of Sex

In the early 1900s, U.S. scientist Thomas Hunt Morgan was studying the genetics of fruit flies. He found that certain traits, such as white eyes and tiny wings, occurred most often in males and only very rarely in females. These traits turned out to be controlled by recessive genes on the X chromosome.

In fruit flies, just as in humans, the X chromosome contains genes not only for female sex characteristics but also for many other traits. But the Y chromosome contains only genes for male sex traits. So if a male fruit fly inherits an X chromosome from his mother with the recessive gene for, say, white eye color, he will have white eyes even though he has only one recessive allele. Since he has only one X chromosome and no corresponding genes on his Y chromosome, he cannot have a dominant red-eye allele to hide the white-eye allele's effects. Females with a white-eye allele on one X chromosome will have red eyes because of the dominant effects of the red-eye allele on the other X chromosome.

The closer two genes are, the more likely they are to be inherited together. If there is a large distance between two genes on the same chromosome, chances are greater that crossing over may occur and they are more likely to be inherited separately. Scientists have used the results of crosses involving linked traits to draw chromosome maps. These maps show the sequence of genes along each chromosome.

Still more genetic variety is added by jumping genes. These are segments of DNA that can move from one spot on the chromosome to another or even to a different chromosome. In some cases, the gene works fine in its new spot. Sometimes, however, switches or modifiers in its new site change the gene's effects or stop it from working. They might result in genetic disorders.

New Discoveries about RNA

RNA does more than just make proteins according to DNA's instructions. Small RNA molecules also help control when and how genes work.

In the early 1990s, researchers at Dartmouth Medical School in New Hampshire were studying mutants of a small worm called *C. elegans*. These mutants stopped developing at an early stage. They found the gene responsible for this problem in 1993. To the researchers' surprise, it coded for an RNA molecule that turned off some of the genes involved in the worm's development. Later, similar genes were found in other organisms, from flies to fish and even humans.

A biologist at the U.S. Centers for Disease Control and Prevention prepares to replicate RNA sequences for an experiment.

Geneticists (scientists who study heredity) believe that hundreds or even thousands of different kinds of small RNA molecules may be in each person's genetic material. They help to control other genes doing a range of jobs in the cell. Some of them are leftover pieces of genes that code for proteins, snipped out when the cell edits these coding genes. Others come from parts of the junk DNA.

A project called the Encyclopedia of DNA Elements (ENCODE) has studied how cells make RNA copies of DNA and translate them into proteins. The scientists found that for each copy of a gene, a cell also makes RNA copies of many other parts of the DNA. These extra RNAs are copies of portions of junk DNA. None of them are translated into proteins.

All Wrapped Up

Looking at a diagram of the DNA double helix, you might think this is the way DNA looks inside cells. That's what it looks like when scientists isolate DNA. Actually, though, the DNA in the nucleus of a living cell is wrapped around spools of proteins called histones. The histones are folded into large loops. So a DNA molecule is actually much longer than the chromosome it forms.

Nearly all the genes on a DNA molecule are bound to histones most of the time, and these genes are turned off. Certain chemicals, such as methyl groups, make the binding to the histones tighter, keeping the genes in a turned-off state. Other chemicals loosen the bonds and allow genes to be uncovered. Only the uncovered genes can be turned on to produce RNA copies and proteins. Chemical signals, together with RNA controls, determine which genes in a cell are working at any moment.

A study reported in 2004 by researchers at the University of California at Santa Cruz used computers to compare human genetic material with that of mice and rats. DNA tends to change a bit from one generation to the next. These changes pile up as new species evolve. Only the most important parts, necessary for survival, stay unchanged. Yet the research team found about five hundred long stretches of junk DNA that were exactly the same in both humans and rodents.

Research on junk DNA is one of the most active fields in science. Scientists are hunting for new RNA-making genes and exploring what the many RNA molecules do. Many of the small RNAs play an important role in an organism's early development. They turn genes on and off in just the right order to help cells travel to the right parts of the body and to form tissues and organs. Other small RNAs help to prevent cancer and heart disease.

chapter four

When the Code Goes Wrong

The DNA in each cell in your body contains an incredible amount of information. If all this information could be recorded on paper, it would fill a thousand books of five hundred pages each. New cells are forming in your body all the time. Each of these cells contains the same set of plans, or DNA. Every time a single cell divides to form two new ones, its DNA is copied—so there are two identical sets, one for each daughter cell.

The copying of DNA in the cell is amazingly accurate. If you copied ten pages from a book and made only one mistake, you would be doing very well. But a cell makes only about one mistake in every *million* pages when it copies its DNA. Just where the copy error occurs on the chromosome makes a big difference. If it happens inside one of the stretches of junk DNA, it may have no effect at all. But if the change occurs in a gene with important instructions, it can cause a big problem.

When a parent cell makes one of these rare errors in copying its DNA, a daughter cell will have a set of DNA that is slightly different from those of the other cells. Such a change in the DNA is called a mutation. The daughter cell will pass on the mutation to its own daughters when it divides, and they may pass it on in turn.

Errors in DNA copying can cause birth defects like extra fingers and toes. This condition is called polydactyly. It is usually corrected with surgery.

Mutations are changes in the plans that the DNA carries. If a mutation occurs in one of the early cells that starts off the life of a new baby, the plans of development may be terribly upset. This may cause problems in the production of important proteins. For example, the baby may be born with missing fingers or toes, or serious diseases can result.

Fixing the "Typos"

Most of the time, DNA copy errors are fixed before they cause harm. Just as an editor would catch and correct the typos in a manuscript, the body has its own editors—enzymes. Special enzymes go on a search-and-rescue mission to quickly find the mistakes and fix them. One enzyme, for instance, looks for damaged or mismatched As, Cs, Ts, and Gs. When it finds one, it cuts it out of the DNA strand. Then another kind of enzyme finds the correct letter and puts it in the right spot, replacing the old one. A third enzyme then makes sure that all the letters are in the right order and connected properly.

Kinds of Mutations

Mutations are changes in the sequence of bases in genes. Mutations can occur in a number of different ways. For instance, the substitution of a single base—replacing the correct base with an incorrect one—may not have much effect. If it changes an amino acid in a key part of a protein, however, it can change the nature of the protein. A number of diseases have been found to result from a change in just one base in a gene.

Some mutations may result in the deletion (removal) of one or more bases. Bases may also be inserted or added to the DNA chain. Unless there is a deletion or insertion of exactly three bases or a multiple of three, the codons after the change are not going to read properly. For example, take the code ATT TAG CAT GAG. If the A in the second codon is deleted, the reading frame of the sequence gets shifted. The message will read ATT TGC ATG AG. All the "words" (codons) after the deletion are garbled, and the message no longer makes sense.

Another type of mutation is known as translocation.

Translocations occur when a piece of a chromosome breaks off and then reattaches—not to where it belongs but to some other chromosome. Depending on where it broke, the effects differ. The genes may work perfectly well in their new location. Or they may be influenced by other genes on the new chromosome, and the way they work may be changed. If a break occurs in the middle of the gene, the whole gene may stop working completely.

Mutations may also involve changes in the number of chromosomes. For instance, things may go wrong in the process of cell division that produces the sex cells. The chromosome sets may not separate properly, causing one sex cell to get an extra chromosome, while another is missing one. If that sex cell joins with one of the opposite sex to start a new life, the cells of the new organism may have three of a particular chromosome or only one instead of the normal pair.

Genetic Disorders

Researchers have identified more than four thousand hereditary diseases and disorders. These conditions are due to changes in the genes and can be passed on from one generation to another. Some involve only one gene, but others involve more than one. In some genetic disorders, a whole chromosome is added or lost.

Single-gene disorders include conditions with just one gene mutation. For example, sickle-cell anemia is a disease that happens when a single letter in the gene for hemoglobin is copied incorrectly. (Hemoglobin is the red-colored chemical in red blood cells.) This small change affects the shape of the

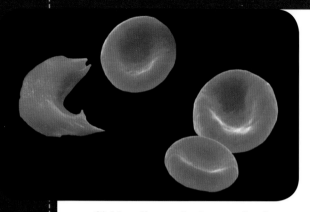

red blood cells, which are needed to carry oxygen throughout the body. Normally these cells are shaped like little doughnuts without the holes. But red blood cells with faulty

Sickle-cell anemia changes the shape of red blood cells. The crescent-shaped cells, like the cell on the left, are fragile and can cause damage to blood vessels.

hemoglobin collapse into a shape like a crescent moon or a sickle. These sickle cells can be damaged easily, and the number of working red blood cells decreases. Sickle cells may also pile up in clumps, clogging blood vessels and damaging them.

How Common Are Genetic Diseases?

Most single-gene disorders are quite rare. But they may be much more common in certain groups of the population. Sickle-cell anemia, for example, affects 1 out of every 500 African Americans. Among Caucasians, the most common genetic disease is cystic fibrosis, in which thick mucus builds up in the lungs and makes breathing difficult. Cystic fibrosis occurs in 1 out of 2,000 Caucasians in the United States, and 1 in 22 is a carrier of the cystic fibrosis gene.

A person can carry the sickle-cell gene without actually having the illness. In fact, carriers of the gene may not even know they have it. However, a child can develop the disease if he or she receives two copies of the mutated gene: one copy from the mother and one from the father. Sickle-cell disease is a recessive trait. It will show up only when two copies of the mutation come together.

Huntington's disease is another genetic illness that involves a single gene mutation. Unlike sickle-cell anemia, however, this mutation is dominant. So a child can get this disease even if only one parent is carrying the Huntington's gene. Huntington's disease is a fatal illness that slowly destroys the parts of the brain that control body movements.

People who are carrying the Huntington's gene may not even realize they have it until years after they have given birth to

This elderly woman suffers from Huntington's disease. People with this disease lose control of the muscles in their face, arms, and trunk. Their arms jerk, and twitching muscles cause them to make unusual faces. They may also have problems with memory.

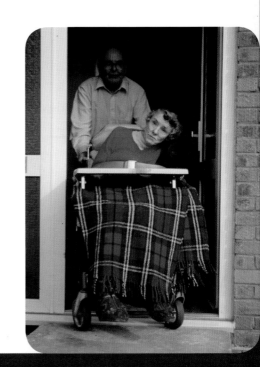

children of their own. Strangely, the defect in the gene (a repetition of the bases CAG) seems to multiply when it is passed down from one generation to the next. This causes symptoms to be more severe and appear at an earlier age, generation after generation.

Single-gene disorders may also be linked to sex. Sex-linked disorders are caused by a mutation on the X chromosome. One example is hemophilia, in which the blood does not clot properly and a person can bleed to death from a minor cut. Hemophilia occurs most often in males. Females can carry a hemophilia gene, but most do not get the disease. Because this is a recessive trait, a female gets it only if she has inherited *two* hemophilia genes, one from each parent. Female carriers can, however, pass this mutant gene down to future generations. As a result, sons and grandsons may get hemophilia.

Some genetic conditions are a result of changes in more than one gene or a combination of genetic and environmental influences. Some common examples are physical conditions such as clubfoot and cleft palate. These disorders tend to occur in families, but they do not show clear patterns of heredity. In fact, it is sometimes hard to tell whether they are really genetic or purely environmental.

Chromosomal disorders develop when there is a problem with an entire chromosome, instead of just one or a few genes. Down syndrome happens when a person receives an extra chromosome. It is the most common example of this kind of mutation.

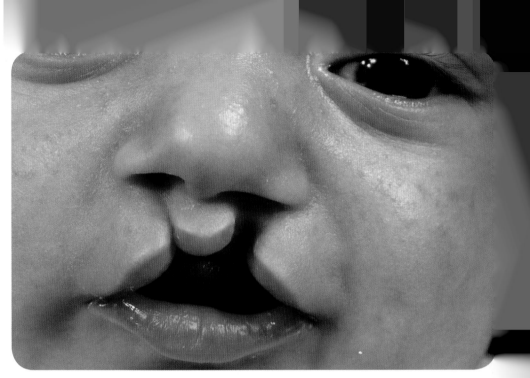

This baby has a cleft lip and cleft palate. The genes that direct the growth of the embryo's face and mouth stopped the growth of the lip and the roof of the mouth before they had closed up correctly. Doctors usually correct this condition with surgery.

Normally, people get two copies of chromosome 21 (one from the mother and one from the father). People with Down syndrome receive three copies (two from one parent and one from the other parent). This happens when the chromosomes were not divided up properly during the cell division that formed the sex cells. So instead of having the usual total of forty-six chromosomes in each body cell, a person with Down syndrome has forty-seven chromosomes.

Down syndrome is apparent at birth, and people with this disorder have distinct physical traits. Developmental disabilities are also a common sign, although they may range from mild to severe. Other physical problems may develop as well.

Genetic Testing

If there were a test that could show whether you are carrying the genes for a deadly disease that could strike you in ten years, would you want to take the test? What about a test that could predict your chances of having a child with some disabling or fatal disorder?

The science of genetics has come a long way since Mendel's time. Genetic testing can determine a person's risk of having genetic disorders later in life. Tests can also show whether or not a couple is likely to have a child with a genetic disorder. Doctors can even check on a baby's health months before it is born, determining whether it has any of several hundred different inherited disorders.

Genetic but Not Hereditary

If you spend too much time out in the Sun without using sunscreen, the DNA in your skin cells may be damaged. The ultraviolet rays in the Sun cause mutations that damage the normal controls over cell growth and division. The damaged skin cells may begin to multiply uncontrollably. They have turned into cancer cells.

Can skin cancer be passed on to children? No, because only the sex cells, sperm and eggs, are involved in forming a baby. Future children would not

Since genes control the production of proteins, genetic diseases usually involve a change that results in a protein that does not work properly or is not produced at all. In some cases, tests for the protein in blood or skin cells can reveal not only people who have the disorder but also people who are carrying the recessive gene for it. Tay-Sachs disease, for example, is a serious illness that results in death at an early age. Babies born with it lack an enzyme called hex-A. Without this key enzyme, a chemical builds up in nerve cells and in time destroys them. Blood tests can show if potential parents have the gene because carriers produce smaller than usual amounts of hex-A.

Doctors can detect chromosome disorders, such as Down syndrome, by looking at the chromosome set of cells from a

get any of the mutated skin cells. So this kind is cancer is not hereditary. It is genetic, though, because it is caused by changes in the genes.

Scientists have found a number of genes that are associated with cancer. Some of these genes, called oncogenes, cause cells to turn "outlaw." Others actually *protect* against cancer. (Cancer results when these protective genes are damaged or lost.) Some of these cancers are hereditary. They develop when oncogenes in the sex cells are passed on to the next generation.

fetus. The test involves drawing out a sample of fluid through a needle inserted into the mother's abdomen. Similar tests can reveal whether the parents are carrying chromosomes with defects that have been linked with genetic diseases.

DNA testing has made it possible to detect far more genetic disorders, both in future parents and in their children. In a blood or tissue sample, researchers use special enzymes that act like chemical scissors to cut up the DNA. This makes fragments of varying lengths. A technique called electrophoresis separates the DNA fragments and sorts them according to length. It makes a banded pattern that looks like a

This diagram shows the method of testing for Down syndrome before a baby is born.

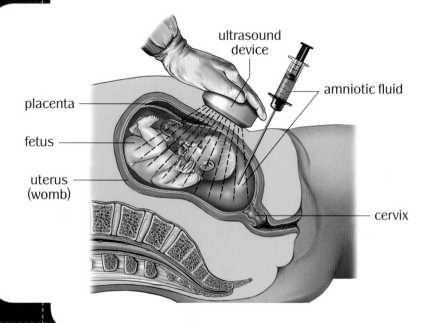

ultrasound device

amniotic fluid

placenta

fetus

uterus (womb)

cervix

DNA

bar code, determined by the group of DNA fragments. Scientists call these fragments restriction fragment length polymorphisms, or RFLPs (pronounced "riff-lips").

Using a special syringe, the scientist inserts DNA fragments into gel in the red tray of an electrophoresis machine. The machine then runs electric current through the gel to separate and sort the fragments.

The RFLP patterns are different for each person (like individual "fingerprints"). But parts of the patterns are similar among members of the same family. Some of them are typically found in people with specific genetic disorders and thus can be used to screen for these disorders.

Restriction enzymes can also be used to snip out defective genes in a sample taken from someone with a genetic disorder. These genes can then be mixed with a blood or tissue sample. If the person being tested has a copy of the gene for that disorder, the test gene lines up with that part of the chromosome and bonds to it.

What Good Is Genetic Testing?

The purpose of genetic testing is to show whether a person carries a mutation that can lead to a serious genetic condition. It does not, however, show whether the person will ever get the disease. The person could be a carrier and pass the trait down to future generations. Environmental influences may also play a role in passing it down.

After electrophoresis, scientists apply a special dye to the gel. The DNA fragments appear as a series of bands. The bands can be photographed and studied.

If genetic testing can't tell you whether or not you will get a disease, then why bother? First of all, if you know that you are at risk, you may be able to spot symptoms right away. For many diseases, early treatment can be a lifesaver. Phenylketonuria (PKU), for example, can be found with a simple chemical test on a spot of urine in a newborn baby's diaper. Someone with PKU does not have the enzyme to handle one of the amino acids commonly found in foods. A toxic product called phenyl ketone builds up in the brain, and the child ends up with developmental problems. But if such a child is identified early and fed a special diet, the child will develop normally.

Genetic testing is also a good tool for people who worry about passing mutant genes to their offspring. If a woman who carries mutant genes marries a man who has a match for one of these genes, any of their children could have a genetic disorder. People who are at risk for a disorder may seek genetic counseling. A genetic counselor will look at the family history and DNA test results. The counselor will also help the clients understand the genetic test results and interpret the risks for passing on the disease. For example, consider a man and a woman who both have a mutant gene for cystic fibrosis. They have a 25 percent chance of giving birth to a child who will receive both copies of the cystic fibrosis gene and, therefore,

Newborn Screening

When you were born, the medical workers ran a lot of tests to make sure you were healthy. One of the tests was probably a genetic test. A drop of blood from a newborn baby's heel can show any risk for hundreds of diseases. Exactly which ones depend on the state where the child was born. Most states have laws requiring newborn screening for certain diseases. About 98 percent of all children born in the United States are tested for PKU, sickle-cell disease, and hypothyroidism. Many states go much further. On the average, newborn screening tests cover four to ten diseases. Hospitals in several states, including New York, test for more than forty genetic diseases.

will develop the disease. This doesn't mean that if this couple has four children, then just one of them will have cystic fibrosis. It means that *each* child has a one in four chance of getting the disease.

Some parents do not want to take a chance on passing on mutant genes to their children. Other options include adoption or in vitro fertilization, in which an egg is fertilized with sperm in a laboratory dish. It is then inserted into a woman's uterus. If the husband's sperm is used, the embryo is tested for the disease gene before implanting. The mother's egg may also be tested and used.

A doctor fertilizes a woman's eggs for in vitro fertilization.

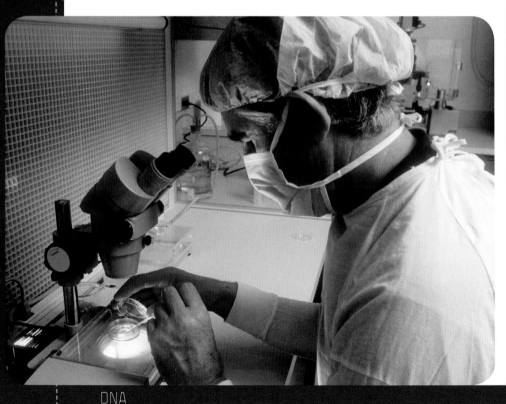

Should people be tested for genetic diseases that can't be cured? Many people say no to tests for Alzheimer's, Parkinson's, and other diseases that may develop in later life. If they can't be cured, they would rather not know their risk. People also worry about possible discrimination. If their medical records include DNA results showing that they *might* get a disabling or fatal disease, will they have trouble getting a job or health insurance?

DNA testing is very expensive. But testing techniques are always improving. Soon the costs may be much more affordable. Treatments are also improving. Already we have ways to slow down the development of conditions that can't yet be cured, such as Alzheimer's, heart disease, and diabetes. If people know about their risks, they might notice early symptoms in time to do something about them. Knowing they are at risk for a disease, people might also choose to support research on cures.

Everything that makes you who you are, from eye color to a tendency for baldness or allergies, is all stored in your DNA. Scientists refer to the total DNA in an organism as its genome. (The term *genome* comes from blending the two words *gene* and *chromosome*.) Researchers believe that if they can figure out the human genome, then they may be able to get to the root of genetic disorders. Then they can design techniques to fix the errors in the code before they turn into a problem.

Focusing on the Human Genome

Can you imagine trying to read the instruction manual that makes up the human genome? It contains more than 3 billion chemical base pairs! But that's exactly what researchers had in mind when the Human Genome Project was created in October 1990. With funding by the U.S. government, the Human Genome Project had one main goal: to map and sequence all the DNA in human chromosomes.

To make a genetic map, researchers needed to figure out which genes belong to which chromosomes and where each gene lies on that chromosome. Then they had to figure out the DNA sequence—the specific order of As, Cs, Ts, and Gs in the entire genome. They aimed to reach their goal by 2005.

Researchers at the Human Genome Project, headed by Francis Collins, began working toward their goal. Meanwhile, another team of researchers, led by J. Craig Venter, was also studying genes, using private funding. Venter had worked on decoding genes for the National Institutes of Health (NIH) but found the methods used at NIH very slow. Frustrated, Venter joined a private research firm that had state-of-the-art equipment to speed up the

Francis Collins (**right**) *listens as J. Craig Venter* (**left**) *speaks at a press conference about the sequencing of the human genome.*

process of identifying the chemical letters in DNA. There, he and his colleagues were able to decode the genome of the first free-living organism—a bacterium.

By 1998 Venter headed a new company, called Celera Genomics, which had powerful gene-sequencing machines. He then set his sights on the human genome. Venter declared that the sequencing would be complete by 2001, four years earlier than the goal of the Human Genome

Personal Portraits

How would you like to know exactly what's in your own personal genetic "instruction book"? In 2001 the complete genomes of two famous genetics researchers were published. Craig Venter worked out his own genome. Nobel Prize winner James Watson got his genome as a present from researchers at 454 Life Sciences and Baylor College of Medicine. The project took two months and cost one million dollars. The researchers believe that in time the cost of mapping a personal genome could come down to about one thousand dollars.

A number of differences existed between the Venter and Watson genomes. And neither of them exactly

Project. So the race was on. Which team would be the first to crack the human genetic code? In June 2000, Venter and Collins independently reached their goals around the same time. Once they figured out the "spelling" of the chromosomes, the next step is to identify the genes and what they do. This is no easy task.

Why is it so important to decode the human genome? Scientists hope that by learning exactly where the genes are and what they do, they will be able to control the actions of key genes. For example, they may be able to turn off

---

matched the general human genome maps that came out in 2000. That's because no two people are exactly alike. Variations of hereditary traits mean differences in the genes. The general human maps from 2000 were averages based on samples from hundreds of people.

In mapping his own genome, Venter found that he is carrying genes that increase his risk for heart disease, blindness, alcoholism, lactose intolerance, high blood pressure, and obesity. Venter says that knowing about these genes has motivated him to exercise and stick to healthy eating habits. Watson found he has some cancer genes, but he says he doesn't want to know if he has a gene for Alzheimer's disease.

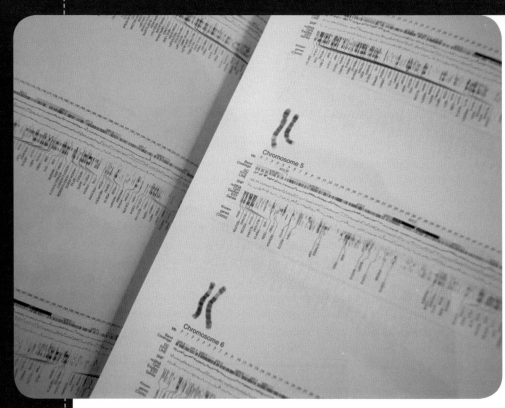

In 2006 the magazine **Nature** *published the sequence of the last chromosome. However, scientists have not finished studying the centromeres on human chromosomes.*

genes that cause obesity or strengthen the signals of those that prevent cancer. Pharmaceutical companies hope to come up with new medicines to fight diseases.

With the ability to map a person's genome, doctors of the not-too-distant future will also be able to make an individual treatment plan for each patient. Knowing what genes the patient has will allow them to choose the drugs that will be the most effective and cause the fewest side effects.

Genomes of Other Species

Since the human genome project began, researchers have studied the genomes of other species as well. They have worked out the genomes for hundreds of kinds of organisms, including bacteria, fruit flies, yeasts, worms, plants, mice, cats, dogs, and elephants.

Scientists have completed the first sequence of a plant, *Arabidopsis thaliana*, a tiny weed related to the mustard plant. It is not a useful crop, but it's easy to study in the laboratory because its genome is small (125 million base pairs compared to our 3 billion). It also multiplies very quickly, growing up to one million plants in a year.

Scientists believe that this plant can be a model for all other plants. Researchers have found 100 genes in *Arabidopsis* that could be used to make new herbicides. Other genes may help plants become resistant to frost and drought. *Arabidopsis* may even help in finding cures for human diseases. Nearly 150 genes in this plant are similar to genes linked with diseases in humans.

Researchers have also worked out the complete sequence of the rice genome, which has about 430 million base pairs. Rice is an important crop for half the world's population, but it lacks some important nutrients. Genetic researchers have been introducing genes to make new varieties of rice with extra nutrients. Golden Rice, for example, is a genetically modified (GM, or changed) kind that contains twenty-three times the usual amount of vitamin A. Eating this rice can help prevent blindness. This is especially important in Asia, where foods rich in vitamin A are not a normal part of the diet.

Researchers hope that the study of mice will be important in working out the human genome. Amazingly, about 80 percent

Gene Count

Before the human genome map was completed, scientists believed that humans had a total of 100,000 genes. The first draft of the human genome investigation suggested that the number is much lower—around 30,000 to 35,000 genes. Later data brought the estimate down further, to about 20,000 to 25,000 genes. By comparison, a roundworm has about 19,000 genes, and the fruit fly *Drosophila* has 13,000 genes. Single-celled bacteria have far fewer genes. *Haemophilus influenzae*, the bacterium sequenced by Craig Venter, has only 1,743 genes, and mycoplasmas, the smallest living things, have fewer than 500 genes.

of the mouse genome is almost exactly the same as the genes in humans. Researchers are tinkering with mouse genes, perhaps eliminating (knocking out) one or changing a base or two. Then they are studying what effects these changes produce. For example, "knockout mice" lacking one of the genes needed to form the eye develop cataracts (a clouding of the eye lens that results in blindness). Once the function of a mouse gene has been revealed, it can be compared to the sequence in the human genome. This may provide insights into human disorders.

Why do some people get sick when exposed to disease germs, while others can fight them off? Researchers have found genes in mice linked to the ability to fight off disease germs. Other mouse genes have been linked to obesity. A tendency toward alcoholism has also been linked to certain genes in mice. The knowledge gained in studying mice can provide a better understanding of these conditions in humans.

Have you ever looked at your own fingerprints? If you press your fingertips against an ink pad and then press them firmly on a piece of paper, you will see patterns of curvy lines, loops, and whorls. Have a friend make his or her own fingerprints. Then compare your fingerprints to your friend's. Can you spot any differences in the patterns?

Fingerprints are like your very own personal ID card. No two people have the same fingerprints. In fact, police have used fingerprinting for identification purposes since the 1890s. Over the years, many criminals have been caught when police officers dusted for prints at the crime scene and matched them with those of a suspect. But what if a criminal wears gloves and doesn't leave any fingerprints? Fingerprints can also be changed through surgery.

These days, criminal investigations are depending more and more on a different kind of fingerprint that cannot be changed—DNA fingerprinting. No two people have the same DNA, except identical twins.

DNA

Positive ID

Earlier we discussed the techniques used to turn a DNA sample into a personal bar code, similar to those you see in supermarkets. Originally, scientists used these personal DNA fingerprints to detect genetic disorders by finding patterns linked to specific traits. In the mid-1980s, DNA fingerprinting started to be used in criminal investigations as well. A sample of DNA can be taken from hair, blood, saliva, sweat, or other bodily materials. (When you

A scientist compares DNA fingerprints using photographs of electrophoresis samples.

turn a doorknob, for example, you leave behind thousands of dead skin cells, which could be used for DNA testing.) If the DNA fingerprint from the sample is identical to the one taken from a suspect, then it is likely that they came from the same person.

DNA fingerprinting has been used to solve many crimes. For instance, the DNA in the dried saliva from a stamp led to the arrest of the Unabomber, Theodore Kaczynski, in 1996. Kaczynski mailed packages containing bombs that exploded when unsuspecting victims opened them. DNA testing has also freed people who have been wrongfully convicted of murder or rape.

DNA fingerprinting can be used to find out whether two people are related to each other. For instance, DNA matches have allowed immigrants to stay in the United States legally when genetic tests showed that they were related to a resident. These tests have also been used in paternity suits, when there is a question of who is really the father of a child.

DNA tests have revealed identities of unknown Vietnam War veterans two decades after they died.

Copy Machine

Sometimes not a lot of evidence is left at a crime scene. There may be just a drop of blood or a single strand of hair. In such cases, the sample may not be big enough for electrophoresis testing. So researchers use the polymerase chain reaction (PCR), which works somewhat like a copy machine. A DNA polymerase, an enzyme involved in making new copies of DNA, is used to copy a small segment of DNA over and over again (a chain reaction). Millions of exact copies are made, giving the testers more material to work with.

Since 1994 the military has been collecting blood and saliva samples from all new members of the armed forces. The samples are stored in freezers and recorded in computer bases. DNA testing can then be used, if needed, to identify soldiers killed in the line of duty.

DNA fingerprinting has also been helpful in identifying victims of natural disasters. DNA tests identified more than 900 people who died in the South Asian tsunami of 2004. The following year, Hurricane Katrina hit the Gulf Coast of the United States, leaving hundreds of unidentified victims. Scientists identified more than 250 victims by matching their DNA to samples from close relatives.

Did You Know?
About 99.8 percent of your DNA is exactly the same as everyone else's. But in a genome of 3 billion letters, even 0.2 percent translates into 6 million separate spellings. The variations in the letter sequences are what make us so different from one another.

The chances of DNA results being inaccurate are one in seventy billion. People are identified by the sequence of base pairs in their DNA. But there are billions of base pairs in the genome, far too many for scientists to test. So how can the results be so accurate? Researchers use only a small number of short segments of the total DNA sequence, but they target those that are known to vary greatly among individuals. When the patterns of these sequences in one sample are identical to those in another sample, they have a match.

DNA Reveals Clues to the Past

DNA testing has become useful for gaining knowledge about organisms that have existed both in the past and in the present. Scientists use DNA testing to classify organisms; to determine evolutionary relationships among animals, plants, and even humans; and to choose mates for captive endangered species.

Researchers have been able to take DNA samples from ancient specimens and compare them to samples from present-day creatures. It is especially helpful when these organisms have been preserved. For instance, ancient insects have been preserved in amber, the hardened resin of certain types of trees.

The investigators wondered if they could match the seedpods to that specific tree using DNA tests. Up to that time, no one even knew whether different trees of the same species had individual DNA fingerprints. A researcher from the University of Arizona in Tucson ran studies on the paloverde trees in the area. He found that each one did have a unique DNA pattern. The DNA from the seedpods in the truck exactly matched the DNA of the damaged tree at the murder scene.

Researchers at the American Museum of Natural History in New York City used DNA testing to study a very large termite found encased in amber dated to about three million years ago. This ancient specimen was found to be closely related to modern termites. In one gene, for example, only nine out of one

The body of this mosquito, trapped in amber around thirty-eight million years ago, contains enough genetic information to study the history of the species.

hundred base pairs differed between the ancient and modern species. Comparisons of DNA also let the researchers trace the ancient termite's evolutionary relationships to modern termites, as well as to other insects, including roaches and praying mantises.

It is rare for animals' flesh and soft tissue to be preserved. However, frozen remains of woolly mammoths have been found in Siberia and Alaska. In the early 1980s, scientists examined genetic material taken from a mammoth. They found that the DNA

In 1999 Russian scientists excavated the remains of this woolly mammoth from the frozen ground of Siberia. The animal died about twenty-three thousand years ago. They used samples from the remains to study its DNA. They also examined the DNA of plant and animal remains found near the mammoth.

in these creatures was more similar to that of Asian elephants than to that of African elephants.

Researchers have compared DNA from bones of Neanderthal fossils with that of modern humans. They found that the Neanderthals were not our ancestors. About 99.5 percent of the bases in the Neanderthal genome are the same as those in humans. But the other 0.5 percent comes to about three million bases—enough for many important differences. These findings suggest that humans and Neanderthals split from a common ancestor about five hundred thousand to six hundred thousand years ago. Apparently, humans and Neanderthals did not interbreed with each other.

Did You Know?
Close to 99 percent of the DNA in our genes is the same as the genetic information of chimpanzees. Chimpanzees are more closely related to humans than to gorillas.

Scientists have also compared the DNA in living people from present-day Europe and Africa. The DNA suggests that Europe was settled about twenty-five thousand years ago by a few hundred people from Africa. Similarities in genetic patterns show that these people all came from the same group of ancestors. The differences reveal how long ago the immigrants to Europe separated from the rest of the African population.

chapter seven

Tinkering with DNA

Since the 1950s, scientists have learned a great deal about how DNA and genes work. They are using their knowledge to try to manipulate the chemicals of heredity. One goal is to fix the defects that produce genetic disorders. Another is to improve on agricultural plants and animals to produce bigger yields or healthier foods.

Tinkering with genes can also provide new sources of disease-fighting drugs and other valuable materials, using specially modified bacteria, plants, or animals. In fact, the original aim of the Scottish researchers who first cloned a sheep was to find ways of mass-producing genetically modified animals without the uncertainties of breeding.

Genetic Engineering

Scientists have learned to engineer living organisms—to change their genes to produce special traits in their offspring. For instance, they have inserted genes into plants to make them more resistant to diseases or to make them able to grow in harsh environments.

Genetically modified corn plants grow in a field in Iowa. They have been altered to resist insects that damage cornstalks.

Scientists have also made genetically modified plants that resist insect damage. This can help to cut down on the use of pesticides, which can be harmful to humans and the environment. For example, organic farmers (farmers who don't use pesticides) have been using a kind of bacteria, called Bt, for pest control. These bacteria are harmless to people and to the environment but poisonous to insects. An insect doesn't die right after taking a bite out of a plant that has been sprayed with Bt. As it starts to digest the food with Bt, the bacteria release a poison that in time kills the pest.

Instead of spraying Bt on plants, genetic engineers have taken the poison gene from the bacterium and inserted it into food crops. For instance, Monsanto has made genetically

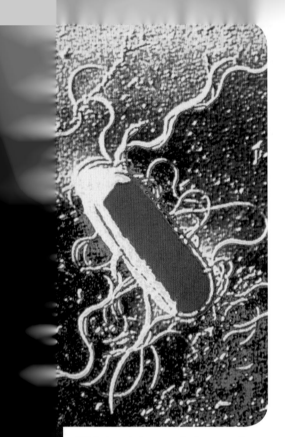

This is a microscopic image of the bacterium Bt. Its full name is Bacillus thuringiensis.

altered potatoes that contain the Bt gene. The company is trying to save potatoes from Colorado potato beetles, which are major pests to the plant.

Monsanto has also genetically engineered corn plants to be resistant to the corn borer. The corn borer is an insect that often damages the inside of the stalk, which cannot be reached by pesticides. Each cell of these genetically engineered plants contains the Bt gene so that the plants are fully protected against insect pests.

Since 1986 thousands of genetically modified plants have been developed around the world. Efforts will most likely continue in years to come. The most common GM foods are soybeans, corn, canola and cottonseed oils, and wheat. As of 2007, more than eight million farmers in seventeen countries were growing GM crops. However, just five countries—the United States, Canada,

Argentina, China, and Brazil—accounted for 98 percent of these GM crops. In Europe, GM foods were banned for six years, until 2004. Strict regulations require that any foods containing GM crops must be clearly labeled, so that people can choose whether to buy them.

Some people object strongly to GM foods. They call them Frankenfoods and say that genetic engineering is unsafe and unproven. The U.S. Food and Drug Administration (FDA), however, says that genetically altered foods are no different from the originals chemically, nutritionally, and in safety.

Another fear is that the genes from GM crops may escape from the farms where they are grown and enter the gene pool of unmodified crops and weeds. Genes for resistance to

A scientist (below) *examines samples of genetically altered crops in a laboratory in Germany.*

insects or herbicides could have harmful effects on helpful insects such as bees and on birds that feed on weed seeds and insects. Researchers are looking for evidence of these wider effects. Local, national, and international communities may eventually have to choose between the benefits of genetic engineering and the possible dangers.

How Gene Tinkering Works

How do scientists change a gene? They use a technique called gene-splicing. Restriction enzymes act as chemical scissors, cutting DNA molecules at certain points. A piece of DNA is taken from an organism and spliced (joined) to a DNA molecule of another organism. DNA that contains pieces from different species is called recombinant DNA. It has genetic material that is different from the original DNA pieces. When recombinant DNA is inserted back into the organism, it changes the organism's traits.

The recombinant DNA is then placed into a bacterium. Some bacteria have small rings of DNA, called plasmids, in addition to their chromosome. They typically code for traits such as resistance to antibiotics. Bacteria sometimes transfer plasmids from one to another. Thus, genes can spread into new populations or species by a kind of natural genetic engineering. Researchers find plasmids useful as small packages for transferring and mass-producing genes.

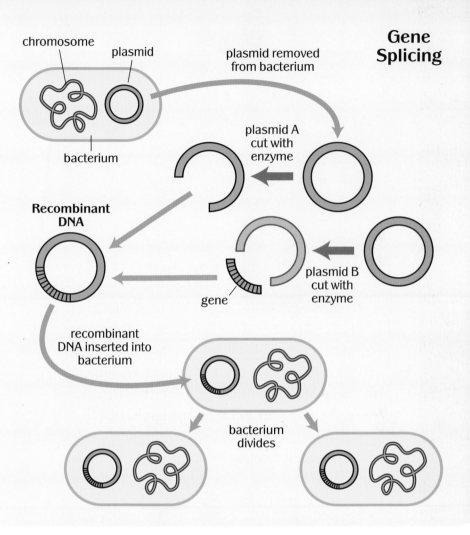

Gene Splicing

chromosome

plasmid

plasmid removed
from bacterium

bacterium

plasmid A
cut with
enzyme

**Recombinant
DNA**

plasmid B
cut with
enzyme

gene

recombinant
DNA inserted into
bacterium

bacterium
divides

*In recombinant DNA work, scientists remove a plasmid from a
bacterium, cut the plasmid open with restriction enzymes, and insert
a gene that has been cut out using the same restriction enzymes. The
plasmid is then put back into the bacterium, and special techniques are
used to multiply the plasmid so that a single bacterium contains many
copies of it. When the bacterium divides, it produces an exact copy of itself,
and each copy contains the plasmids, along with their inserted genes.*

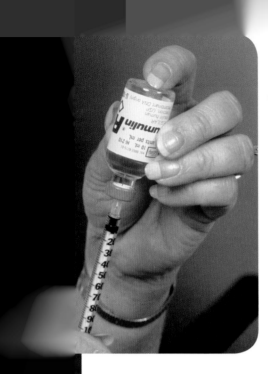

A nurse draws recombinant DNA insulin from a vial. Insulin was the first drug produced by recombinant DNA technology.

The specially treated bacteria become little factories, producing large numbers of bacterial cells that have the human gene. The bacterial factories provide a way to make large amounts of proteins that normally are present in only tiny amounts. For example, researchers have used bacteria to make human insulin used to treat diabetes. Bacterial cells have also been used to make medicine to treat people with hemophilia.

"Pharming"

Genetically engineered bacteria growing in huge tanks are only one source of useful biochemicals (chemicals made by living organisms). In this fast-growing industry, genes for human proteins can also be inserted into farm animals such as sheep, cows, pigs, and goats. Often the genetic changes are designed so that the animals secrete the human proteins in

Researchers at the University of Guelph in Ontario, Canada, have created genetically altered pigs that produce less phosphorus in their manure than other pigs. Phosphorus from pig manure can pollute rivers and kill fish.

their milk. The milk can be collected without harming the animals, and the human proteins can easily be separated from it. Since farm animals can thus be used to make pharmaceuticals (drugs), this kind of genetic engineering is often called pharming.

Animals whose genome contains inserted genes from another species are called transgenic animals. Transgenic pigs are already being used to make human insulin. Transgenic sheep are a source of human growth hormone and a protein used to treat a lung disease called emphysema.

Genetic changes in cattle genes might produce reduced-fat milk or milk that is better for people who cannot digest the milk sugar, lactose. Scientists are testing various blood proteins from the milk of transgenic animals. Some

> ## Did You Know?
>
> The Scottish company that produced Dolly, the cloned sheep, sells human proteins secreted in the milk of transgenic sheep.

can be used to remove blood clots blocking important arteries to treat anemia (a lack of red blood cells). Others work to stop bleeding in people who lack some of the blood-clotting proteins that help close up wounds.

One of the most unusual pharming products is spider silk, secreted in the milk of transgenic goats. Spider silk is the strongest material known—five times stronger than steel. Silk proteins from transgenic goats with some spider genes can be spun to make thin thread for surgical stitches, clothes that don't wear out or tear, and even bulletproof vests.

In addition to serving as living factories for producing human proteins, animal pharming can also lead to better farm animals. Australian researchers,

A Genetic Shortcut

For thousands of years, people have been aware that living things pass down their traits from one generation to the next, even though they didn't know about genes and how they work. Dog breeders, for example, carefully selected animals with specific traits to produce offspring with the traits of their parents. That's how many dog breeds, such as dachshunds, Great Danes, and Chihuahuas, have evolved. Modern farmers even select and crossbreed many kinds of fruits and vegetables we eat every day.

These transgenic goats from Nexia Biotechnologies produce a protein that breaks down chemical weapons. Transgenic animals often look no different from other animals.

for example, have made genetically modified sheep that grow more wool. A genetically engineered hormone has been developed to cause sheep to shed their fleece. This lets sheep raisers harvest the

It can take some time for desired traits to appear, however. To speed up the process, genetic engineers have figured out which genes govern specific traits. Then in a laboratory, they chemically insert the desired gene into an animal or plant. So genetic engineering is not really new but rather a kind of shortcut for what animal and plant breeders have been doing all along—selecting for favorable genes.

American and Canadian fisheries harvest millions of sockeye salmon every year. Genetic modification can provide fish for human consumption while protecting the species from overfishing.

wool without having to shear the sheep.

Another Australian research team is working on a gene-splicing method to protect sheep from flies that lay their eggs in sheep's skin. They have spliced a gene for a tobacco protein into the sheep's sweat glands, hoping that the toxic chemical it produces will kill off burrowing fly larvae.

Growth hormone genes from a variety of species, from fish to chickens, mice, and humans, have been inserted into trout, salmon, and other fish. With the extra growth hormone, the transgenic fish grow much faster. Genetically modified salmon, for example, grow twice as fast as usual and can be raised on fish farms, without having to spend part of their life in the ocean. Wild salmon are among the species threatened with extinction, and doctors recommend salmon as part of a healthy diet for humans. Genetic engineering can help increase the supply of this important food source.

Fish Genes in Strawberries?

A video on the Internet shows a tearful mother talking about the death of her child. Little Annie died of an allergic reaction after eating a GM strawberry. Annie was allergic to fish, not strawberries, but the fruit contained fish genes added to make the strawberry plants more resistant to cold weather. This is a really scary story, but it isn't true. Strawberries containing fish genes have never been sold.

Researchers have been trying to make tomatoes and strawberries that can survive frosts, however. And they did try inserting genes for "antifreeze proteins" from Arctic flounders, but the plants were not frost resistant. In more recent studies, researchers have been using genes from Antarctic plants to make cold-hardy strains of wheat and other crops.

Other researchers have used genetic engineering to produce healthier pigs. Researchers inserted a gene from the roundworm *C. elegans* into pig embryo cells and then cloned a litter of piglets. The worm gene helps cells turn a kind of fat called omega-6 fatty acids into the heart-healthier omega-3 fatty acids. The researchers plan to use their cloned pigs for studies on nutrition and heart disease, but they could also be bred as meat animals. Ham, pork, and bacon could become part of a heart-healthy diet.

Medical researchers hope that transgenic pigs will provide a source of replacement tissues and organs for transplanting into humans. Usually xenotransplants (*xeno-* means "foreign") are rejected by the body's immune system. But scientists are trying to "knock out" the gene for an enzyme that puts certain chemicals on the surface of pig cells. These surface chemicals are the main "tags" that human body cells reject as foreign. Eliminating them can reduce the danger of rejection. Researchers are also adding genes for proteins that will make the pig tissues more humanlike. Organ transplants from "humanized" pigs into monkeys survive much longer than those from untreated pigs.

Gene Therapy

Hereditary diseases develop as a result of errors in copying the complete set of genes from parents to their children. As scientists learned more about genes and developed ways of working with them, the next step seemed logical: supply healthy genes to take over the jobs of the defective or missing ones. This kind of treatment is known as gene therapy. Using it, doctors may be able to treat genetic disorders and diseases where no treatment exists.

Effective gene therapy requires getting the new genes into the patient's cells and making sure they work properly. Recombinant DNA techniques provide ways of making or modifying genes. They

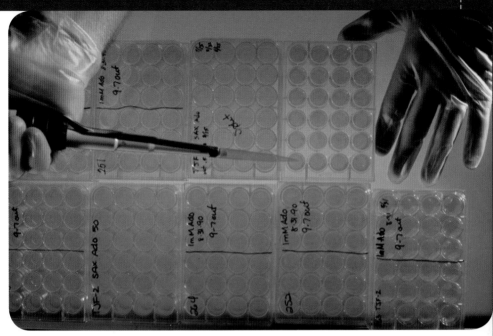

A scientist prepares samples of cells containing corrected genes. These cells will be used in gene therapy.

can even be mass-produced in cultures of bacteria. Harmless viruses may be used to carry genes into cells. Sometimes bits of "naked DNA" are injected directly into cells taken from the patient and then put back into the body. The new genes may also be placed inside liposomes—tiny balls of a fatty material. These liposomes are small enough to pass through the tiny openings in the membrane around the cell's nucleus.

Medical experts believe that gene therapy is a promising approach. However, it has caused some controversy. During the 1990s, some patients undergoing gene therapy showed little or no improvement in their conditions. Then in September 1999, a gene therapy patient, eighteen-year-old Jesse Gelsinger, was being treated for a genetic liver disease. He died due to complications of the therapy.

At Case Western Reserve University in Cleveland, Ohio, researchers accidentally made their own real-life supermice in November 2007. They really wanted to study an enzyme called PEPCK-C. This enzyme helps cells produce energy.

The scientists tinkered with mouse genes to build a special PEPCK-C gene that makes the enzyme mainly in muscle tissue. By adding this gene to the DNA of mouse embryos, they bred a strain of mice that have a lot more energy than usual. The supermice can run on a treadmill for six hours without stopping, covering close to 4 miles (6 kilometers). Normal mice are so tired they need to take a nap after only 0.1 mile (0.2 km). The

Despite this tragedy, there have been some small successes. At Children's Hospital in Philadelphia, for example, gene therapy helped children with hemophilia make a blood-clotting protein they lacked. French doctors reported promising tests of gene therapy for children with a rare genetic defect that disables the body's immune system against infectious diseases and cancer.

PEPCK-C mice are more active in their cages too. Researcher Parvin Hakimi says that when she opened their cage, it was like taking the lid off a popcorn popper.

The supermice have big appetites, eating 60 percent more than normal mice. But they stay thin, with only half the usual body weight and one-tenth as much body fat. They live longer than normal mice, and they stay strong and healthy longer. A PEPCK-C mouse that is two and a half years old can run twice as fast as a normal mouse less than a year old. They can breed longer too. One PEPCK-C mouse gave birth to a litter when she was almost three years old, when normal mice would be dying of old age.

Yoda (left) *and Princess Leia* (right) *are genetically modified mice. Yoda lived to be four years old, a very long time for mice.*

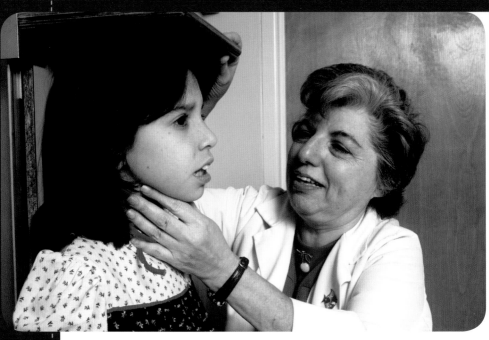

A doctor measures the height of a girl undergoing treatment with recombinant DNA growth hormone. This treatment uses genetically altered cells to stimulate growth in children who are much smaller than normal. It can also treat other diseases, including multiple sclerosis and complications associated with acquired immunodeficiency syndrome (AIDS).

In Boston, researchers have been working with heart disease patients. These patients suffered from chest pain due to clogged arteries that prevented enough blood from reaching the heart muscle. Injecting genes that cause new blood vessels to grow into the patients' hearts provided new blood supply routes and relieved their chest pains.

The most encouraging gene therapy results so far have been in the treatment of cancer. Many cancers are caused by damage to genes that regulate the way cells grow and multiply. Radiation, from the ultraviolet (UV) rays of the Sun to "hard radiations" such as X-rays and gamma rays, can cause such damage. Genes can also be damaged by carcinogens—cancer-causing chemicals such as those found in cigarette smoke—and by errors in copying DNA when cells divide. One important gene that prevents cancer is called p53. It normally works to detect problems in a cell. If a cell has become cancerous, p53 directs it to commit suicide.

Researchers believe that defects in p53 are involved in as many as 50 to 75 percent of all cancers in humans. In gene therapy experiments, scientists have inserted copies of the p53 gene into viruses that were first stripped of their disease-causing parts. The viruses carrying p53 were then used to infect cancer patients, who had lung cancer or tumors of the head and neck. In many patients, the tumors stopped growing, shrank, or even disappeared.

In 2006 researchers at the National Institutes of Health in Bethesda, Maryland, used a different gene therapy approach. They were treating patients with melanoma that had spread from the skin to other parts of the body. They inserted genes for proteins that recognize cancer cells into some of the patients' own white blood cells. When these transgenic cells were injected into the patients, they went after the patients' cancer cells. In two patients, the tumors shrank.

Gene therapy is also promising for treating disease due to defects in bone marrow cells. Bone marrow makes both red blood cells and the various white blood cells. In 2002 researchers used gene therapy to cure sickle-cell disease in mice. Afterward, researchers begin working on ways to replace the defective gene in human sickle-cell patients.

Meanwhile, an international group of scientists has been working on another bone-marrow-related disease, called X-CGD (X-linked chronic granulomatous disease). People with this disease have trouble fighting off disease germs because their white blood cells lack a key enzyme. The researchers used a harmless virus to carry the missing gene into two patients' bone marrow. To their surprise, the patients not only began making the enzyme, but three other genes in the blood-forming cells were also turned on. The numbers of disease-fighting white blood cells tripled and started killing bacteria and fungi. The patients were able to stop taking the daily antibiotics they had needed to stay healthy.

Doctors announced another gene therapy success in 2007. At Moorfields Eye Hospital in London, England, doctors used gene therapy to cure a hereditary type of childhood blindness. In this disease, a defective gene causes the retina (the light-sensitive layer of cells at the back of the eyeball) to break down. Inserting healthy copies of the gene into patients' retina cells lets them see clearly again.

The gene therapy treatments tried so far have not helped everyone. Sometimes their effects were only temporary. But researchers are working to improve the treatments. This is just one of the ways our growing knowledge of DNA is expanding our ability to improve living conditions and to save lives.

Glossary

alleles: different forms of the same gene. For example, one allele of the gene for eye color produces blue eyes and another allele produces brown eyes.

amino acids: building blocks of proteins

biochemicals: chemicals found in or produced by living organisms

carcinogen: a cancer-causing substance

carrier: an organism with one allele of a recessive trait. The organism does not show the trait but can pass on the gene for it to offspring.

cell: the basic unit of life

cell division: the process by which one cell divides into two

centromere: a round structure joining two identical chromosomes formed after a cell has copied its DNA in preparation for cell division.

chromatids: a chromosome and its identical copy, joined together near the middle by a centromere. Chromosomes exist in this form when a cell is getting ready to divide.

chromosomes: tiny threadlike structures that carry DNA, found within the nucleus of a cell

clone: a cell, cell product, or organism that contains genetic material identical to the original

codon: a three-letter sequence of nucleotides in the messenger RNA chain that codes for a specific amino acid in the production of a protein molecule

crossing over: the process by which maternal and paternal chromosomes exchange genetic material, creating new combinations of genes

cytoplasm: the substance between the cell membrane and the nucleus (or the nuclear body in bacteria)

deletion: a type of mutation that occurs when one base or more is absent from the DNA chain

DNA (deoxyribonucleic acid): the substance that carries the hereditary instructions for making proteins

dominant: referring to the form of a trait that appears even if the organism has only one copy of the gene for it

electrophoresis: a technique that sorts DNA fragments by moving them at different speeds along a layer of gel under the influence of electric current

enzyme: a special protein that helps make chemical reactions take place

exon: a portion of a gene containing the code for assembling amino acids into a protein

fertilization: the process by which egg and sperm nuclei join

fetus: a developing human in the period from three months after conception to birth

genes: chemical units that determine hereditary traits passed on from one generation of cells or organisms to the next

gene-splicing: isolating a piece of DNA and joining it to a DNA molecule of another organism

genome: the total amount of DNA in an organism

genotype: a combination of alleles that is responsible for a trait

histone: a protein that binds to DNA in the nucleus and is involved in turning genes on and off

hybrid: a cell that forms as a result of joining cells from two different species

insertion: a type of mutation that occurs when one or more bases are added to the DNA chain

intron: a segment of DNA within a gene that does not code for protein production

jumping genes: segments of DNA that can move from one position on the chromosome to another or even to a different chromosome

junk DNA: portions of DNA in the genome that do not code for proteins and have no apparent function

linked traits: traits determined by genes that are close together on the same chromosome and thus are usually inherited together

liposomes: tiny balls of fatty material that can transport genes into cells

mitochondrion: energy-generating structures in cells

mutation: a chemical change in a gene, which may produce a new trait that can be inherited

nucleotide: a building block of DNA or RNA. It consists of a nitrogen base, a sugar, and a phosphate

nucleus: the control center of a cell, which contains its hereditary instructions and is surrounded by a membrane separating it from the rest of its contents

oncogene: a gene that causes cells to grow uncontrollably, resulting in cancer

ovum: a female sex cell (egg cell)

PCR (polymerase chain reaction): a technique in which a special enzyme is used to copy a small segment of DNA over and over, giving the testers more material to work with

phenotype: the visible characteristics of an organism

plasmid: a strand or loop of DNA that exists independently of the chromosome in bacteria or yeasts

recessive: referring to the form of a trait that does not appear unless the organism has inherited two copies of the gene for it, one from each parent

recombinant DNA: DNA that contains pieces from different species

replication: the process by which DNA reproduces itself

restriction enzymes: chemical scissors that cut up DNA

RFLPs (restriction fragment length polymorphisms): DNA fragments obtained when chromosomes are cut with restriction enzymes. When separated by electrophoresis, they form a pattern that looks like a bar code.

Selected Bibliography

Aldridge, Susan. *The Thread of Life: The Story of Genes and Genetic Engineering*. New York: Cambridge University Press, 1996.

BBC. "European Union Lifts GM Food Ban." *BBC News*. May 19, 2004. http://news.bbc.co.uk/2/low/europe/3727827.stm (November 13, 2007).

Coghlan, Andy. "'Junk' DNA Makes Compulsive Reading." *NewScientist.com*. June 13, 2007. http://www.newscientist.com/article/mg19426086.000-junk-dna-makes-compulsive-reading.html (October 23, 2007).

Cornell Cooperative Extension. "Fish-Gene Strawberries and Tomatoes." *Genetically Engineered Organisms: Public Issues Education Project*. N.d. http://www.geo-pie.cornell.edu/media/fishberries.html (November 13, 2007).

Feuer, Jim. "Gene Therapy Appears to Cure Myeloid Blood Diseases in Groundbreaking International Study." *Cincinnati Children's*. March 31, 2001. http://www.cincinnatichildrens.org/about/news/release/2006/3-gene-therapy.htm (November 14, 2007).

Frank-Kamenetskii, Maxim D. *Unraveling DNA: The Most Important Molecule of Life*. Reading, MA: Perseus Books, 1997.

Freudenrich, Craig C. "How Cloning Works." *How Stuff Works*. March 26, 2001. http://www.howstuffworks.com/cloning.htm (October 23, 2007).

Gajilan, A. Chris. "Mapping Own DNA Changes Scientist's Life." *CNN.com*. September 4, 2007. http://www.cnn.com/2007/HEALTH/09/04/dna.venter/index.html (September 5, 2007).

Galbincea, Barb. "Scientists Create a Mighty Mouse in the Lab." *Newark (NJ) Star Ledger*, November 4, 2007.

Gillespie, David. "Pharming for Pharmaceuticals." *Learn.Genetics*. 2007. http://learn.genetics.utah.edu/features/pharming/ (November 13, 2007).

HowStuffWorks."How DNA Evidence Works." *How Stuff Works.* January 18, 2001. http://www.howstuffworks.com/dna-evidence.htm (November 1, 2007).

Jefferis, David. *Cloning: Frontiers of Genetic Engineering.* New York: Crabtree Publishing Company, 1999.

Lawrence Berkeley National Laboratory. "Neanderthal Genome Sequencing Yields Surprising Results and Opens a New Door to Future Studies." *Science Daily.* November 16, 2006. http://www.sciencedaily.com/ releases/2006/11/061116083223.htm (October 23, 2007).

Lozano, Juan A. "Scientist Gets Own Personal Genome Map." *MSNBC.com.* May 31, 2007. http://www.msnbc.msn.com/id/18968279/ (October 18, 2007).

Lurie, Karen. "Junk DNA." *ScienCentralNEWS: Making Sense of Science.* July 20, 2004. http://www.sciencentral.com/articles/view.php3?type =article&article_id=218392305 (November 16, 2007).

Mestel, Rosie. "Murder Trial Features Tree's Genetic Fingerprint." *NewScientist.com.* May 29, 1993. http://www.newscientist.com/article/ mg13818750.600-murder-trial-features-trees-genetic-fingerprint-.html (November 9, 2007).

NCI. "New Method of Gene Therapy Alters Immune Cells for Treatment of Advanced Melanoma; Technique May Also Apply to Other Common Cancers." *National Cancer Institute.* August 31, 2006. http:// www.cancer.gov/newscenter/pressreleases/MelanomaGeneTherapy (November 14, 2007).

Oliver, Rachel. "All About: GM Rice." *CNN.com/asia.* October 30, 2007. http://edition.cnn.com/2007/WORLD/asiapcf/10/15/eco.about.rice/ index.html (November 13, 2007).

Pollack, Robert. *Signs of Life: The Language and Meanings of DNA.* New York: Houghton Mifflin Company, 1994.

Ridley, Matt. *Genome: The Autobiography of a Species in 23 Chapters.* New York: Fourth Estate, 2000.

Smith, Michael. "Transgenic Pigs May Bring Home Heart-Healthy Bacon." *MedPage Today.* March 27, 2006. http://www.medpagetoday.com/ Cardiology/Prevention/tb/2934 (November 14, 2007).

Sohn, Jie-Ae. "Donor Pigs May Save Human Lives." *CNN. com.* February 23, 2005. http://edition.cnn.com/2005/ TECH/02/23/spark.pigs/index.html (November 14, 2007).

Tagliaferro, Linda, and Mark V. Bloom. *The Complete Idiot's Guide to Decoding Your Genes.* New York: Alpha Books, 1999.

Watson, James. *DNA: The Secret of Life.* New York: Alfred A. Knopf, 2004.

Woodhouse, Janette, ed. "Antarctic Genes Incorporated into Frost-Resistant Wheat." *Food Processing Online.* October 15, 2007. http://www.foodprocessing.com.au/latest_news/ article.asp?item=13351 (November 2, 2007).

For Further Information

Books:

Balkwill, Fran, and Mic Rolph. *Gene Machines*. New York: Cold Spring Harbor Laboratory Press, 2002.

———. *Have a Nice DNA*. New York: Cold Spring Harbor Laboratory Press, 2002.

Cefrey, Holly. *Cloning and Genetic Engineering*. New York: Children's Press, 2002.

Claybourne, Anna. *The Usborne Introduction to Genes & DNA: Internet Linked*. London: Usborne Publishing, 2006.

Fridell, Ron. *Decoding Life: Unraveling the Mysteries of the Genome*. Minneapolis: Twenty-First Century Books, 2005.

———. *Genetic Engineering*. Minneapolis: Lerner Publications Company, 2006.

Johnson, Rebecca L. *Genetics*. Minneapolis: Twenty-First Century Books, 2005.

Meyer, Anna. *The DNA Detectives: How the Double Helix Is Solving Puzzles of the Past*. New York: Thunder's Mouth Press, 2006.

Platt, Richard. *Forensics*. New York: Kingfisher Knowledge, 2005.

Walker, Richard. *Genes and DNA*. New York: Kingfisher Knowledge, 2003.

Websites

The Basics on Genes and Genetic Disorders
http://www.kidshealth.org/teen/your_body/health_basics/genes_genetic_disorders.html
This website for kids covers all the basic information on genes and genetic disorders.

The Cloning of Dolly and Other Mammals
http://www.biology.iupui.edu/biocourses/Biol540/12cloningfullCSS.html
A Purdue University site made for college students has great pictures and links to the major events in cloning research.

Crack the Code

http://nobelprize.org/educational_games/medicine/gene-code/how.html

This is a Nobel Foundation site with information on the genetic code, Marshall Nirenberg, DNA structure, and DNA-RNA-Protein. You can play games such as "Double Helix" and "Crack the Code."

DNA

http://www.pbs.org/wnet/dna/

This site has features based on PBS episodes, "The Secret of Life," "Playing God," "The Human Race," "Curing Cancer," and "Pandora's Box," with articles on DNA structure, the genome project, GM foods, gene therapy, solving crimes with DNA, and the future of genetics. Videos include the first experiments in genetic engineering and the genome project. A timeline and a 3-D DNA Explorer are included.

The DNA-o-gram Generator

http://www.thinkbiotech.com/DNA-o-gram/

Send someone an e-mail message translated into DNA code. The site also has "DNA from A to Z," with links to articles on the many uses of DNA, from alien communication and bioremediation to Lego creations, music, and nanotechnology to xenotransplantation, yogurt, and zinfandel (a table wine).

DNA Workshop: You Try It

http://www.pbs.org/wgbh/aso/tryit/dna/

A PBS *Science Odyssey* site has background information on DNA and protein synthesis and interactive programs that take you through the steps of copying DNA and making proteins.

Gene Almanac

http://vector.cshl.org/

The website of the DNA Learning Center at Cold Spring

Harbor Laboratory has features on "DNA from the Beginning" and "Your Genes, Your Health," including animations, audio, and video.

Genetic Science Learning Center

http://gslc.genetics.utah.edu/

This website includes features on basic genetics, genetic disorders, and genetics in society, with a special section for students and teens.

How DNA Works

http://science.howstuffworks.com/dna4.htm

This site provides a simple explanation of what DNA does, with colorful illustrations. It also includes links to DNA structure, how proteins are built, mutations, and lots more.

Human Genome Project Information

http://www.ornl.gov/TechResources/Human_Genome/home.html

The official website of the Department of Energy Human Genome Program has many news articles, frequently asked questions, research reports, ethical discussions, fact sheets, and links.

Kids Genetics

http://www.genetics.gsk.com/kids/dna01.htm

This is a kid-friendly guide to DNA, genes, heredity, and genetic diseases produced by GlaxoSmithKline; with interactive features including a DNA-building game to play online.

Understanding Genetics

http://www.thetech.org/genetics/

The site of the Tech Museum of Innovation has features on "Genetics and Health," "Zooming into DNA" (microscopic images), "What Color Eyes Will Your Children Have?" "Ask a Geneticist," and "Genetics in the News."

Index

Photo Acknowledgments

The images in this book are used with permission of: © Edward Kinsman/Photo Researchers, Inc., p. 4; © Joe Vogan/SuperStock, p. 5; © Laura Westlund/Independent Picture Service, pp. 6, 9, 14, 21, 34, 79; © A. Barrington Brown/Photo Researchers, Inc., p. 10; © Dr. Tim Evans/Photo Researchers, Inc., p. 11; © Biodisc/Visuals Unlimited, p. 19 (left); © Steve Allen/The Image Bank/Getty Images, p. 19 (right); © iStockphoto.com/digitalskillet, p. 23 (top); © Scientifica/RML/Visuals Unlimited, p. 23 (bottom); © 3D4Medical.com/Getty Images, p. 25; © Getty Images, p. 27; © Bill Hauser/Independent Picture Service, p. 28; © Time & Life Pictures/Getty Images, p. 32; © Superstock, Inc./SuperStock, p. 35; Centers for Disease Control and Prevention Public Health Image Library/James Gathany, p. 39; © Mediscan/Visuals Unlimited, p. 43; © Dr. Stanley Flegler/Visuals Unlimited, p. 46; © Conor Caffrey/Photo Researchers, Inc., p. 47; © Dr. M.A. Ansary/Photo Researchers, Inc., p. 49; © Nucleus Medical Art/Visuals Unlimited, p. 52; © Scientifica/Visuals Unlimited, p. 53; © Science VU/NIH/Visuals Unlimited, p. 54; © Yvonne Hemsey/Getty Images, p. 56; © Alex Wong/Newsmakers/Getty Images, p. 59; © Vo Trung Dung/CORBIS SYGMA, p. 62; © SIU/Visuals Unlimited, pp. 67, 80; © Kjell B. Sandved/Visuals Unlimited, p. 71; © Reuters/CORBIS, p. 72; © Kent Foster/Visuals Unlimited, p. 75; © Alfred Pasieka/Photo Researchers, Inc., p. 76; © Peter Ginter/Science Faction/Getty Images, p. 77; © University of Guelph, Ontario, Canada, p. 81; © Sean O'Neill, Nexia Biotechnologies, Inc., p. 83; © Brandon D. Cole/CORBIS, p. 84; © Richard T. Nowitz/Alamy, p. 87; Richard A. Miller/University of Michigan Medical School, p. 89; © Science VU/Genentech/Visuals Unlimited, p. 90.

Front cover: © Michael Dunning/Photographer's Choice/Getty Images.

About the Authors

Dr. Alvin Silverstein is a former professor of biology and director of the physician assistant program at the College of Staten Island of the City University of New York. Virginia B. Silverstein is a translator of Russian scientific literature.

The Silversteins' collaboration began with a biochemical research project at the University of Pennsylvania. Since then they have produced six children and more than two hundred published books that have received high acclaim for their clear, timely, and authoritative coverage of science and health topics.

Laura Silverstein Nunn, a graduate of Kean College in New Jersey, began helping with the research for her parents' books while she was in high school. Since joining the writing team, she has coauthored more than eighty books.